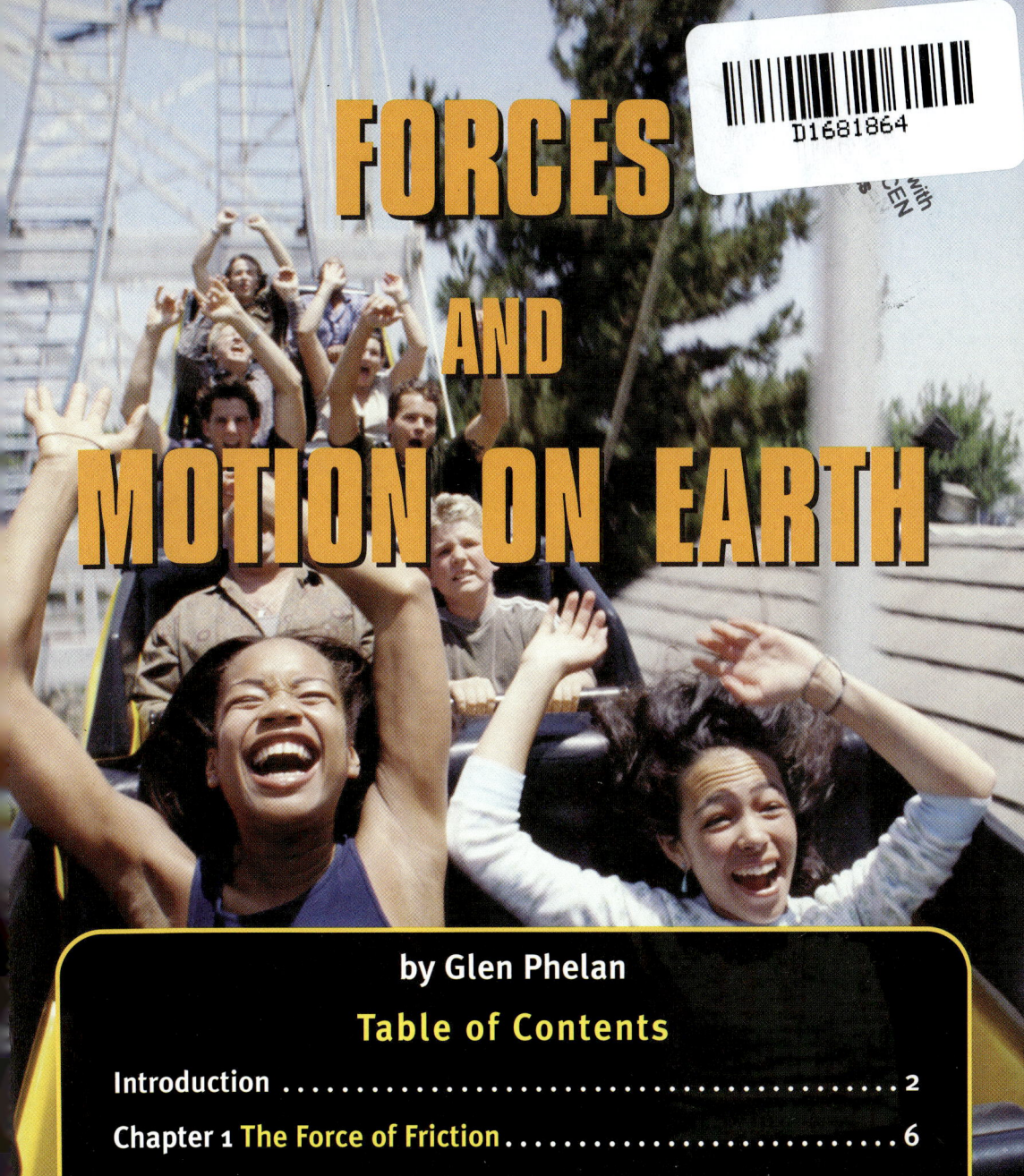

FORCES AND MOTION ON EARTH

by Glen Phelan

Table of Contents

Introduction	2
Chapter 1 **The Force of Friction**	6
Chapter 2 **The Force of Magnetism**	12
Chapter 3 **The Force of Gravity**	18
Chapter 4 **Balanced and Unbalanced Forces**	24
Conclusion	30
Glossary	31
Index	32

Introduction

"Keep your balance," you tell yourself. You crouch low on your skateboard as you begin to roll downhill. Faster and faster you go. The wind is blowing hard in your face now. Will you have enough speed to make it up the other side of the ramp? Yes! With a turn of your body, you work the skateboard up and down the curved walls. What a wild ride! And what a fun way to explore the science of **motion**.

You may not be an expert skateboarder, but you experience all kinds of motion every day. Motion is any change in an object's position. When you raise your hand in class, you change your hand's position—you move it. When a flag blows in the wind, the flag's position keeps changing as it waves back and forth.

We live in a world of constant motion. On your way home from school, you might notice a hundred things moving. But *why* do they move? And *how* do they move?

◀ Raising your arms is an everyday motion, as is a flag blowing in the wind. ▼

▲ A skateboarder is in constant motion.

INTRODUCTION

It's All About Forces

Think about flying a kite. You hold it up with one hand and grab the string with the other. You run and let go of the kite. It moves higher and higher as the string unwinds. Up in the sky, the kite sways back and forth. It dives, it climbs, it spins in circles. What causes all those motions? Forces do.

A **force** is a push or a pull. Whenever you see motion—something moving—you know that pushes and pulls are at work. Think of the kite again. The push of the wind, which is moving air, lifted the kite high into the sky. The wind continued to push the kite in different directions. You controlled some of that motion by pulling on the string.

▲ Forces—pushes and pulls—make the kite move.

Forces make objects start moving. Forces also make objects speed up, slow down, change direction, and stop. Suppose you give a soccer ball a kick to start it moving. The kick is a push—a force. It makes the ball roll across the grass. Then other forces cause the ball to slow down and stop.

Read on to learn about the many forces we experience every day on Earth. Then you'll be able to explain the motions shown in these pictures.

▲ What is being pushed in these pictures? What is being pulled?

CHAPTER 1

The Force of Friction

THUMP! The BMX bike lands hard at the bottom of the dirt hill, but the racer keeps her balance and continues pedaling. She's in the lead with one lap to go. She powers up the next hill and zooms over the top. Will she make the sharp curve at the bottom? She lands with a bang, then leans to the left. The tires press against the ground and kick up a cloud of dirt. She leaves deep tire tracks in the ground and races toward the finish line.

Why didn't the wheels slide out from under the bike at the sharp turn? The answer is **friction** (FRIHK-shuhn). Friction is a force that happens when one object rubs against another object.

Friction ▶ between the tires and the ground keeps the bike on the track but sends the dirt flying.

If friction is a force, where are the pushes or pulls? When two objects rub against each other, they are actually pushing against each other. This pushing creates friction. It keeps the objects, such as the tire and the ground, from sliding past each other easily.

Now suppose that instead of riding on dirt, the BMX racer was riding on ice. What do you think would happen at the sharp turn? You're right—it would be a wipe out! The bike would slide like a hockey puck. That's because smooth surfaces, such as ice, produce less friction than rough surfaces, such as the dirt trail.

It's a Fact

Friction happens because the high spots of rough surfaces snag on each other. All surfaces have some amount of roughness. Even a piece of highly polished metal is rough when seen under a microscope.

CHAPTER 1

Friction All Around

Anywhere you look, you can see friction at work. Even when you walk, friction is produced between the soles of your shoes and the ground. Friction keeps you from slipping, so that you can push off and step forward.

You are probably using friction right now in several ways. Are you sitting in a chair? Friction keeps you from sliding off. When you write with a pencil, friction makes some of the pencil lead rub off onto the paper. Wherever things are rubbing, or even just touching, friction is acting between them.

▼ **You use friction in many ways to ride a bike.**

THE FORCE OF FRICTION

Pedal Power

How do you use friction on a bike? Hop on to find out.
1. You push against the pedals to move the wheels.
2. The wheels push against the ground and you roll forward.
3. The rubber grips on the handlebars increase friction with your hands.
4. A squeeze of the hand brakes makes the brake pads rub against the wheel.
5. Friction between the brake pads and the wheel slows the bike.

Friction between you and the air also slows you down. This friction is called **air resistance** (AYR rih-ZIHS-tuhns). As you move, air particles push against you. You have to keep pedaling to overcome air resistance and friction between the tires and the pavement.

It's a Fact

Air resistance, like any other friction, produces heat. It's not enough heat to feel when you ride a bike. But when the space shuttle re-enters Earth's atmosphere, the heat from air resistance is so great that the shuttle glows.

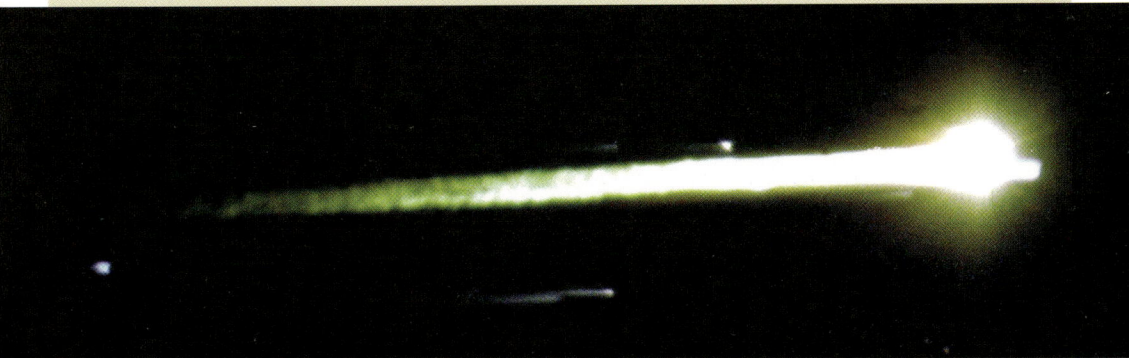

More Friction—or Less?

Sometimes you want to increase friction—for instance, when you are rock climbing hundreds of feet above the ground. Rubber-soled shoes provide more friction than smooth-soled shoes and allow climbers to grip the rocks better.

Similarly, the tread on a car's rubber tires increase friction with the road. This lets the car slow down, turn, and stop safely. Can you imagine how dangerous driving would be if car wheels were made of steel, like those on a train?

Sometimes you want to reduce, or decrease, friction. That's what oil does in a car's engine. The engine has dozens of moving parts. Many of them rub together very quickly. The friction between the parts can wear them down. It also produces a lot of heat that can ruin the engine. Oil reduces friction by forming a slippery film between the moving parts. What other machines use oil or grease to reduce friction?

▲ **Rubber-soled shoes grip better than smooth-soled shoes.**

THE FORCE OF FRICTION

Imagine
Suppose friction was suddenly "turned off" for an hour. How would it affect motion? How would it affect what you're doing right now?

Hands-on Experiment
How Ball Bearings Work

Small metal balls called ball bearings help reduce friction between two surfaces. How do they work?

What You'll Need
- 2 identical pie plates
- 10–20 marbles

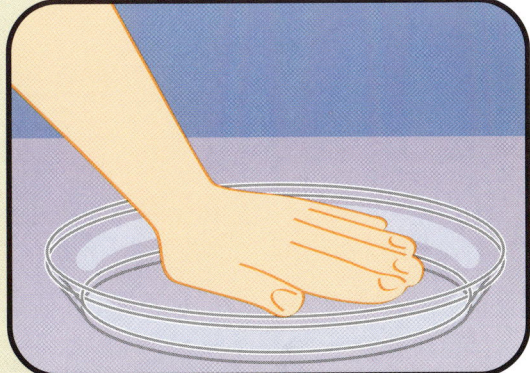

What To Do
1. Set one pie plate inside the other. Try to spin the top plate.
2. Remove the top plate. Put the marbles in the bottom plate.
3. Set the other plate on top of the marbles. Try to spin the top plate.

What Do You Think?
1. How did the marbles change the force needed to overcome friction?
2. Think of two examples where ball bearings would be useful.

11

CHAPTER 2

The Force of Magnetism

It's a clear, dark night. You look up at the sky to admire the stars. Suddenly, the sky begins to glow. A curtain of red, blue, and green light shimmers before your eyes. The black night has turned into a fantastic light show!

This colorful display takes place in the far northern and southern parts of Earth. In the north, it is called the northern lights, or aurora borealis (uh-ROH-rah BOR-ee-ah-lihs). In the south, it is called aurora australis. What causes an aurora? The same force that holds papers onto your refrigerator door—**magnetism**.

The northern lights are caused by magnetism. ▶

Magnetism is a force that attracts, or pulls on, things that contain iron. An object that has magnetism is called a **magnet**. Magnets come in all shapes and sizes—from horseshoes to bars and dots.

No matter what the shape and size, every magnet has two poles, or ends. One pole is called the north pole. The other pole is the south pole.

The force of magnetism is strongest near the poles of a magnet. You can see that in the picture. This magnet was placed near tiny bits of iron. The magnet pulled on the iron bits to create the pattern shown. Where did most of the iron bits go?

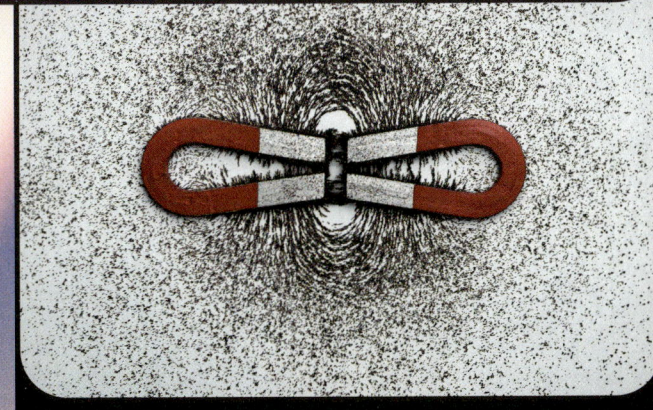

▲ Bits of iron gather at the poles, where magnetism is strongest.

CHAPTER 2

Magnetic Fields

Suppose you spill a box of paper clips all over the floor. What's a fun, quick way to pick them up? Use a magnet! A magnet attracts paper clips because the clips are made of steel, and steel is made from iron.

Now suppose you place a magnet at one end of a table and a paper clip at the other end. The paper clip doesn't move. Why? The paper clip is outside the magnet's **magnetic field** (mahg-NEHT-ihk FEELD).

A magnetic field is the area around a magnet where its magnetism acts. If you place the paper clip inside the magnetic field, the paper clip moves toward the magnet. Large, powerful magnets have large magnetic fields. Smaller, weaker magnets have smaller magnetic fields.

▲ Every magnet has two poles. A magnetic field surrounds a magnet.

▲ Earth has two poles, the North and South Poles.

 point   Think About It

Compare the diagram on this page with the picture on page 13. Can you tell where the magnetic field is in the picture?

14

THE FORCE OF MAGNETISM

Everyday Science

Magnets are all around. You probably have some on your refrigerator that are holding up notes. But did you know that magnets are inside your refrigerator, too? Motors that run refrigerators, vacuum cleaners, and other machines use magnets.

Hands-on Experiment

What things in your home or school contain iron? Get a magnet and find out what objects are attracted to it. (Remember, steel has iron in it.) Use the items listed here, record your findings in the table, and compare it with your classmates' results.

Item	Contains Iron?	
	Yes	No
Quarter	☐	☐
Dime	☐	☐
Nickel	☐	☐
Penny	☐	☐
Spoon	☐	☐
Fork	☐	☐
Doorknob	☐	☐
Key	☐	☐

CHAPTER 2

Earth is a huge magnet. It has magnetic north and south poles. It also has a huge magnetic field that extends out into space. Tiny particles from the sun travel through space and reach Earth's magnetic field. They get pulled toward the poles. The particles then hit gas particles in Earth's atmosphere and give off light. That's what makes auroras, like the one shown on pages 12 and 13.

And because Earth is a huge magnet, you never have to worry about being lost in the woods—as long as you have a map and a compass. The compass needle is a magnet that always points to Earth's magnetic north pole. If you know where magnetic north is, you can figure out every direction: north, south, east, and west.

▲ A compass works because Earth is a huge magnet.

16

THE FORCE OF MAGNETISM

Hands-on Experiment
Make A Compass

It's easy to make a compass. All you need is a magnet and a way to let it move freely.

What You'll Need

- bar magnet • cork • bowl of water • masking tape

What To Do

1. Tape the magnet to the top of the cork.
2. Carefully place the cork into the bowl of water so that the cork floats. Make sure the magnet doesn't get wet.
3. Let the cork turn in the water until it comes to a stop. Note which end of the magnet points north. If you don't know which way is north, ask your teacher or an adult.
4. Take the cork out of the water. Stick a piece of masking tape on the end of the magnet that pointed north.
5. Place the cork back in the water. See if the magnet points north again.

What do you think?

1. How is this compass like a compass you can buy?
2. How could you make a compass without using water?

CHAPTER 3

The Force of Gravity

Nothing beats the summer heat like a cool waterslide. You climb to the top then sit down. The water is rushing all around. You push off and let out a loud yell. Down you go. Why down? The same force that makes your pencil fall when it rolls off the desk—**gravity**.

Gravity is a force that pulls any two objects together. For example, a pencil falls because Earth is pulling the pencil toward it. This pulling force is gravity. Earth is pulling on you, too. Gravity between you and Earth keeps you on the ground. If you jump up, gravity pulls you back down.

▲ The force of Earth's gravity pulls you down the slide.

Like any force, the strength of gravity can vary. It can be so weak that you can't feel it, or so strong that you can't escape it. The strength of the pull of gravity between two objects depends on the **mass** of the objects. Mass is the amount of matter, or material, an object is made of. The greater the mass is, the stronger the pull of gravity.

Think of the falling pencil again. Earth is pulling on the pencil as it falls by your side. Your body also is pulling on the pencil because gravity acts between any two objects. But Earth has a lot more mass than you do, so its pull is a lot stronger. The pencil falls toward Earth, not toward you.

It's a Fact

When Earth pulls on a falling pencil, the pencil pulls on Earth with the same amount of force. Then why doesn't Earth rise toward the pencil? Actually, it does! But the motion is too small to notice.

◀ When an object falls, it is being pulled by the force of gravity.

CHAPTER 3

Gravity and Weight

"This backpack weighs a ton!" You may have said that on your way home from school. You could have also said, "Earth sure is pulling hard on this backpack!"

That last sentence makes sense because **weight** is a measure of the pull of gravity on an object. When you step on a scale to weigh yourself, you are finding out how much Earth's gravity is pulling on you. Now suppose you put a kitten on the scale. The kitten weighs much less than you do. Why? The kitten has less mass than you do. So Earth pulls on it with less force, and it weighs less.

1. Solve This

Most people in the United States and the United Kingdom measure weight in pounds. But scientists measure weight in newtons (N). A medium-sized apple is 1 newton, or about 0.2 pounds. If you cut an apple in four equal slices, about how much would each slice weigh in newtons?

THE FORCE OF GRAVITY

Weight and Mass

You may know by now that weight and mass are related. But they are not the same. For one thing, mass is measured in kilograms, not pounds or newtons. To show how they are different, let's go to the moon.

The moon is smaller than Earth and has less mass. So the force of gravity is less than on Earth. In fact, the moon's gravity is only about one-sixth of Earth's gravity. That means the moon pulls on an object with only one-sixth the force that Earth would pull on it. So an astronaut who weighs 160 pounds on Earth would weigh one-sixth of that, or about 27 pounds, on the moon. But the astronaut's mass doesn't change. He still has the same amount of matter.

> ## 2. Solve This
>
> Suppose astronauts collected a rock that weighed half a pound on the moon. How much did it weigh when they got back to Earth?

21

CHAPTER 3

Which Falls Faster?

You hold a bowling ball at your waist. A friend holds a volleyball at the same height. The balls are about the same size. You both let go of the balls at the same time. Which one hits the ground first?

The bowling ball is much heavier than the volleyball. It has much more mass. So the bowling ball falls faster and hits the ground first, right? Wrong! Gravity makes all objects fall with the same speed as long as no other forces affect the objects. The bowling ball and the volleyball hit the ground at the same time.

They Made A Difference

About 400 years ago, the Italian scientist Galileo (gah-lih-LAY-oh) showed that all objects fall with the same speed. He rolled balls of different masses down a ramp. He was one of the first people to test his ideas by doing experiments. Since then, experiments have become an important part of science.

THE FORCE OF GRAVITY

What if you drop a feather and a bowling ball at the same time? Will they hit the ground together? You probably know they won't. The ball drops quickly while the feather drifts down slowly. That's because other forces besides gravity affect the objects. Air resistance, for example, slows the feather more than the ball.

But what if there was no air? Then the feather and ball should fall at the same speed. In 1971, Apollo 15 astronaut David Scott did an experiment to prove that idea. On the airless moon, he dropped a feather and a hammer. As predicted, they hit the moon's surface at the same time.

Hands-on Experiment

See for yourself how gravity makes objects fall at the same speed. Get two objects that have close to the same shape and size, but are different weights. You might use two kinds of coins or two kinds of balls. Hold the objects up and let them go at the same time. Watch what happens.

CHAPTER 4

Balanced and Unbalanced Forces

"Ready, set, pull!" The tug-of-war begins. Everyone on both teams is pulling with all their might. Yet no one is moving closer to the line. Both teams are pulling with a lot of force. But they are pulling with the *same amount of force* and in *opposite directions*. The forces are equal, or balanced. When **balanced forces** act on an object, the object does not move.

What happens if one team pulls with more force than the other team? The forces are now unequal and unbalanced. The teams and the rope move in the direction of the stronger pull. When **unbalanced forces** act on an object, the object moves or changes its motion.

Everything around you involves balanced and unbalanced forces. For example, hold this book up while you read. The upward force of your hands balances the downward force of gravity. So the book doesn't move. Now lower the book. You are not pushing up with as much force, but gravity still pulls down with the same amount of force as before. The forces are unbalanced and the book moves down.

3. Solve This

In a tug-of-war, Team A pulls with a force of 1,250N. Team B pulls with a force of 1,585N. Which team wins? How much more force does the winning team pull with?

CHAPTER 4

Combining Forces

By now, you may realize that most objects have many forces acting on them at the same time. Let's count some of the forces acting on you when you move a wheelbarrow:

1. You pull up on the handles.
2. You push against the ground with your feet.
3. Friction acts between your shoes and the ground.
4. Friction acts between the wheel and the ground.
5. The wind pushes you to one side.
6. You push back against the wind.
7. Gravity is constantly pulling you and the wheelbarrow down.

What forces ▶ are acting on the man and the wheelbarrow?

26

BALANCED AND UNBALANCED FORCES

With all these forces pushing and pulling at you, how do you get anywhere? The answer is that the forces combine. When the forces combine, some of them cancel each other out completely or partly. The amount of force that remains causes motion.

Sometimes it's easy to tell all the different forces acting on an object. For example, you can almost feel the pushes and pulls of the raging water in the picture below. The people also push and pull with their paddles to avoid dangerous rocks and whirlpools. What other forces are acting on the raft?

Talk About It
Think of an action that you did today. Turn to a partner and describe the different forces that acted on you.

▲ Rafters push and pull to fight the forces of the rushing water.

CHAPTER 4

The direction of a force is just as important as the amount of force. If you and a friend want to move a heavy snowball, does it make sense to push in opposite directions? No, you would push in the same direction. That way, your forces work together and it's easier to move the snowball.

Have you ever tried to push open a window while leaning over a piece of furniture? It can be difficult because the window "sticks." That's because only part of your force is pushing the window up. The rest is moving sideways. That pushes the window frames together and increases their friction. Next time, try moving the furniture out of the way. Then you can get close enough to push straight up.

▲ It is easier to push a big snowball if you combine forces.

BALANCED AND UNBALANCED FORCES

Careers in Science

Do you enjoy building models and making things? Do you like to take things apart and figure out how they work? Then civil engineering (SIHV-uhl ehn-jih-NEER-ing) might be the career for you. Civil engineers design bridges, dams, roads, and other structures. Civil engineers must understand all the forces that act on structures in order to build them safely. To become a civil engineer, you have to study science and math and earn a college degree in engineering. As a civil engineer, you might work for the government, a private company, or start your own engineering company.

Conclusion

Every move you make is caused by one or more forces. Among these forces are friction, magnetism, and gravity. Friction happens when one object rubs against another object. Magnetism is a force that attracts things made of iron. And gravity is a force that pulls any two objects together.

Usually more than one force acts on an object at a time. If the forces are balanced, the object will not move. It only moves when the forces are unbalanced.

Now that you know more about forces, use the concept map shown here to help explain the motions in the pictures on pages 4–5.

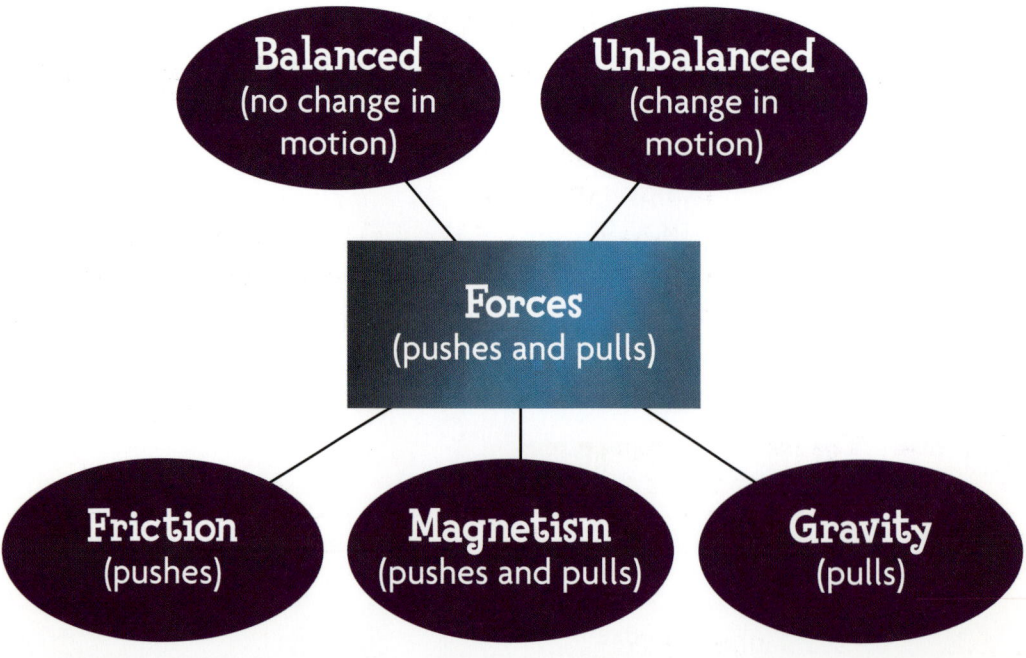

Glossary

air resistance — (AYR rih-ZIHS-tuhns) friction between an object and the air (page 9)

balanced forces — (BAHL-uhnsd FOR-sihs) forces that act equally on an object but in opposite directions (page 24)

force — (FORS) a push or a pull (page 4)

friction — (FRIHK-shuhn) a force that happens when one object rubs against another object (page 6)

gravity — (GRAHV-ih-tee) a force that pulls any two objects together (page 18)

magnet — (MAHG-neHt) an object that has magnetism (page 13)

magnetic field — (mahg-NEHT-ihk FEELD) the area around a magnet where its magnetism acts (page 14)

magnetism — (MAHG-nih-tihz-uhm) a force that attracts things made of iron (page 12)

mass — (MAHS) the amount of matter, or material, an object is made of (page 19)

motion — (MOH-shuhn) any change in an object's position (page 2)

unbalanced forces — (UN-bahl-uhnsd FOR-sihs) forces that result in an object moving or changing its motion (page 24)

weight — (WAYT) a measure of the pull of gravity on an object (page 20)

Solve This Answers

1. **Page 20:** .25N
2. **Page 21:** 3 pounds
3. **Page 25:** Team B wins; 335N

Index

air resistance, 9, 23
balanced forces, 24–25, 30
ball bearings, 11
compass, 16–17
force, 4–7, 12–13, 18–19, 23–24, 26–30
friction, 6–11, 26, 30
Galileo, 22
gravity, 18–23, 25–26, 30
magnet, 13–17
magnetic field, 14
magnetism, 12–17, 30
mass, 19, 21–22
motion, 2–5, 24, 27
newton (N), 20, 21, 25
northern lights, 12
poles, 13–14, 16
Scott, David, 23
unbalanced forces, 24–25, 30
weight, 20–21, 23